Alien Facts #8

BY ZEESHAN MAHMUD

A lasso, technically a **lariat** or **reata**, works via a counter-intuitive physics trick where the spinner must constantly roll the rope between their thumb and forefinger to prevent internal torsion from collapsing the loop. Beyond ranching, the lasso was a lethal **primary weapon of war** for the Huns, Scythians, and Sasanian Persians, who used plaited thongs to drag armored enemies from horses. In 2018, Will Roberts set the bizarre record for the most people—**13 individuals**—standing inside a single spinning lasso. In 2025, the lasso continues to be defined by high-speed feats, such as the record for 100 "Texas skips" (jumping through a spinning loop) in one minute, while its cultural history includes Native

Americans using them to unhorse Spanish conquistadors and the fact that "lasso" is almost always used as a verb by professional cowboys, who simply call the tool a "rope".

20 Bizarre & Mind-Blowing Lasso Facts

1. **Weaponized Thongs:** Ancient tribes like the Sagartians carried only a dirk and a lasso made of plaited thongs as their entire war kit.
2. **The Honda:** The small, reinforced eyelet at the end of the rope that creates the "noose" is technically named a **honda**.
3. **Marine Roots:** The word *reata* (lariat) originally referred to ropes used to bind ship masts.
4. **Robo-Cowboy Law:** Physicists found a loop only stays open if exactly **75% of the rope** is used in the circle itself.
5. **100-Skip Limit:** The current human speed limit for "Texas skips" (jumping through a lasso) is **100 per minute** as of 2025.
6. **Human Hoop:** Will Roberts fit **13 people** (plus himself) inside one spinning lasso in 2018.
7. **Sasanian Elite:** The elite Aswaran cavalry of the Sasanian Empire carried lassos as standard combat gear alongside swords.
8. **Internal Tension:** If you don't roll the rope in your fingers, it will "fight" you and tangle due to accumulated twists.

9. **Lasso of Truth:** Wonder Woman's lasso was inspired by its creator's invention of the **systolic blood pressure test** for lie detection.
10. **Native Resistance:** Native Americans were so proficient they frequently lassoed **Spanish Conquistadors** right off their saddles.
11. **The Hocking Knife:** Before the lasso was perfected, Mexican ranchers used a **crescent blade on a pole** to disable cattle by the hocks.
12. **African Vaqueros:** Some of the first professional "cowboys" in North America were enslaved Africans who refined roping techniques in Mexico.
13. **Spinning Threshold:** A flat loop requires a minimum of **1.4 turns per second** to stay open against gravity.
14. **Crucial Waxing:** To maintain its stiff shape, a modern lariat is often soaked in **piping hot wax** during manufacturing.
15. **Ranch vs. Rodeo:** A "ranch rope" can be up to **100 feet long**, while rodeo ropes are kept short (30 feet) for speed.
16. **Bulgarian Horsemen:** In the 1205 Battle of Adrianople, Bulgarian horsemen used lassos to snatch Crusaders from their horses.
17. **South American Bolas:** Unlike the single-loop lasso, the **bola** uses three weighted strands to entangle prey.
18. **The "Poet Lariat":** Legend claims the fictional Pecos Bill was the first to use a lasso to "tame the wilder members of the herd".

19. **Ambassadors of Rope:** In the 1930s, a high school group called the "Jefferson Lassos" performed for Eleanor Roosevelt.
20. **Pro-Soccer Skill:** On the show *Ted Lasso*, the cast had to prove they could actually play soccer before being hired.

CAN AI REPLICATE CHEKOV?

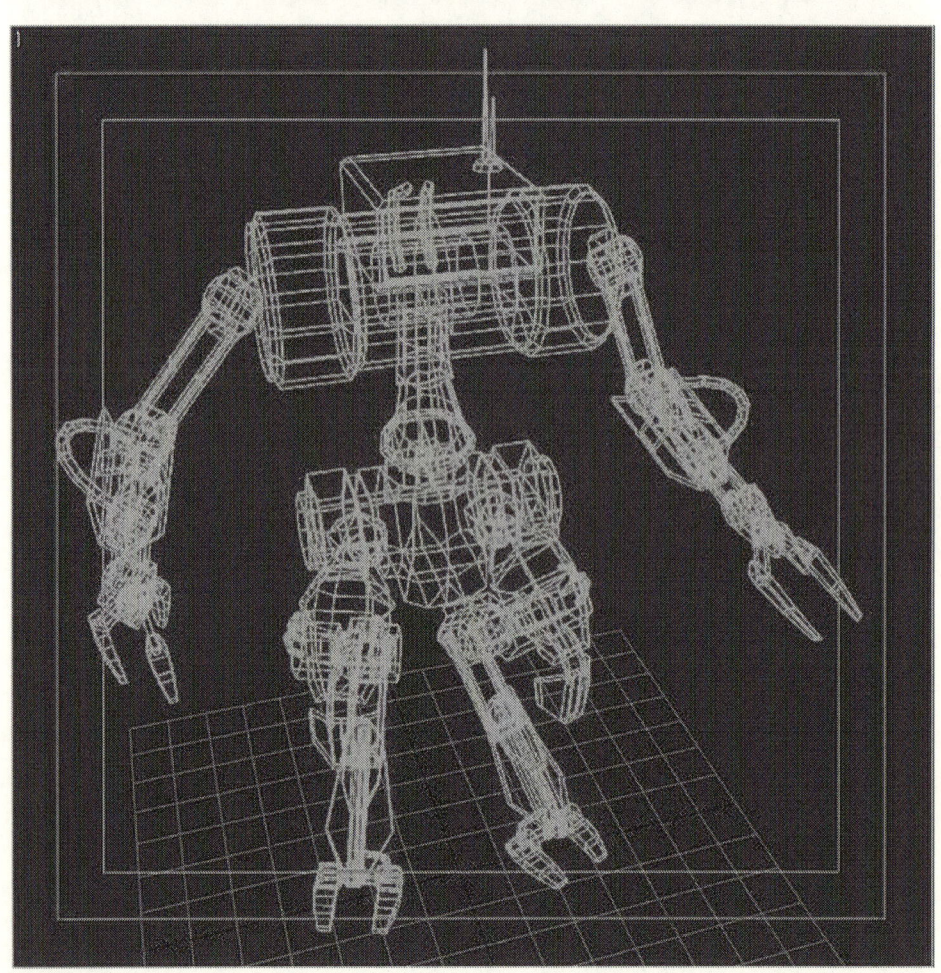

AI is capable of mimicking Anton Chekhov's technical prose style but struggles significantly with replicating his profound psychological subtext and "extreme brevity". While modern Large Language Models (LLMs) can effectively clone Chekhov's vocabulary, syntax, and principles—such as the famous **"Chekhov's Gun"**—they often fail to grasp the nuanced emotional ambiguity and irony that define his masterpieces like *The Cherry Orchard* or *The Lady with the Pet Dog*.

Beyond the Gun: Can AI Replicate the Soul of Chekhov?

Introduction

Anton Chekhov once wrote that the role of an artist is not to solve a problem but to state it correctly. As generative AI evolves from reactive chatbots into autonomous "agentic" systems, the literary world is grappling with whether an algorithm can truly "state" the human condition with Chekhovian grace. While AI can effortlessly replicate a writer's surface-level idiosyncrasies—such as Chekhov's clinical objectivity and preference for realistic, dialogue-heavy narratives—it consistently falls short of the "subtle nuances of the human mind" that make his works timeless.

- **Surface Mimicry vs. Subtextual Depth:** Current AI tools like the Famous Writer Style Mimic can analyze tone and sentence structure to produce original text that "sounds" like Chekhov. However, research indicates that AI still underweights complex emotional themes like guilt, self-destruction, and manipulation, leading to predictable storytelling that lacks the psychological density of human-authored classics.
- **The "Robo-Chekhov" Experiments:** Efforts to create fully AI-generated adaptations of Chekhovian plays, such as *The Harmfulness of Tobacco*, have faced significant hurdles; synthetic actors often struggle with the emotional weight, and language models sometimes fail to maintain the necessary long-term discourse coherence.
- **A Collaborative Future:** Rather than replacing the "Father of the Short Story," AI in 2025 is increasingly used as a "co-pilot" for writers to brainstorm outlines or explore new theatrical forms. Platforms like ReelMind.ai now offer AI-generated dramatic interpretations of *The Cherry Orchard*, allowing creators to analyze these works through new visual and narrative lenses while still relying on human expertise for deep contextual analysis.

Ultimately, while AI can replicate the mechanics of a Chekhovian story, the "beautifully simple" connection to the human psyche remains a uniquely human frontier.

The cogwheel, or gear, evolved independently across several ancient civilizations as a fusion of two simple machines: the wheel and the lever. While its exact origin is debated, the earliest archaeological evidence of man-made gears dates to 4th-century BCE China, where they were utilized in complex mechanisms like the "South Pointing Chariot" to maintain a consistent directional indicator. Simultaneously, the Greek mechanics of the Alexandrian school in the 3rd century BCE, including polymaths like Archimedes, significantly advanced gear technology for power transmission in watermills and irrigation. The most sophisticated ancient application discovered is the Antikythera mechanism (circa 150–100 BCE), a Greek astronomical calculator containing at least 30 bronze gears with triangular teeth. Historically, these early cogs were often made of wood—specifically maple—and were technically wooden teeth fitted into a "mortise wheel" before metal gears became standard during the Industrial Revolution.

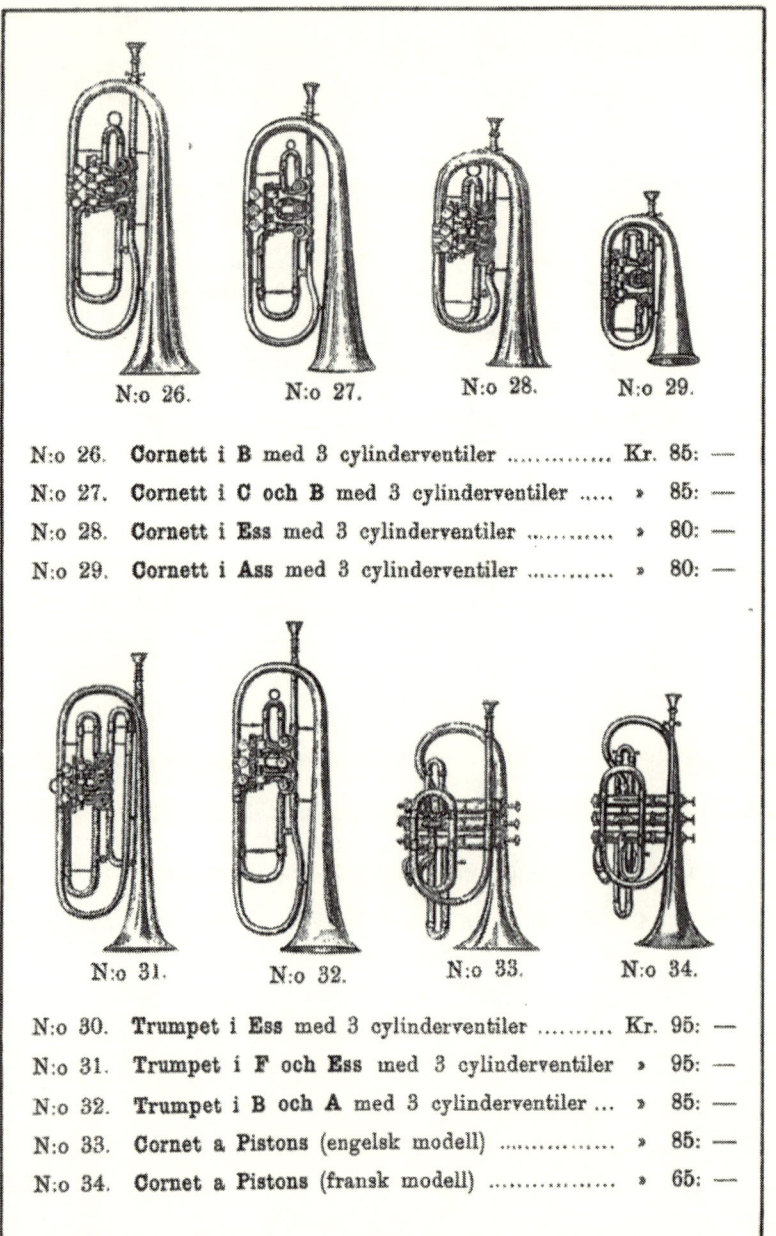

N:o 26. **Cornett i B** med 3 cylinderventiler .... Kr. 85: —
N:o 27. **Cornett i C och B** med 3 cylinderventiler ..... » 85: —
N:o 28. **Cornett i Ess** med 3 cylinderventiler .... » 80: —
N:o 29. **Cornett i Ass** med 3 cylinderventiler .... » 80: —

N:o 30. **Trumpet i Ess** med 3 cylinderventiler .... Kr. 95: —
N:o 31. **Trumpet i F och Ess** med 3 cylinderventiler » 95: —
N:o 32. **Trumpet i B och A** med 3 cylinderventiler ... » 85: —
N:o 33. **Cornet a Pistons** (engelsk modell) .... » 85: —
N:o 34. **Cornet a Pistons** (fransk modell) .... » 65: —

The trumpet family is categorized into over 12 distinct variations, each differing in key, bore shape, and specialized utility. While the standard B♭ trumpet is the most recognized, professional and historical needs have created a wide spectrum of instruments.

The most mind-blowing fact about *20,000 Leagues Under the Sea* is that the number in the title refers to **horizontal distance traveled**, not depth. If the submarine *Nautilus* were actually 20,000 leagues deep, it would be roughly 60,000 miles down—placing it nearly **three times the diameter of the Earth** and a significant portion of the way to the Moon.

20 Bizarre & Rare Jules Verne Facts Original Polish Nemo: Captain Nemo was originally a Polish nobleman seeking revenge against Russia for killing his family, but Verne's publisher forced the change to an Indian prince to avoid offending the Russian book market. **Title Plurality:** The original French title, *Vingt mille lieues sous les mers*, uses "Seas" (plural), which was dropped in many English translations, contributing to the depth vs. distance confusion. **Prophetic Tech:** Verne described electric submarines in 1870, nearly **25 years before** the first functional battery-powered models were launched in the 1880s. **The First "Nemo":** The name "Nemo" is Latin for **"No One,"** a direct allusion to Odysseus's trick against the Cyclops in Homer's *Odyssey*.

Also...

- **Giant Squid Myth:** When the book was published, the existence of the giant squid was still unverified and considered a myth by many scientists.
- **Diving Suit Freedom:** Verne's description of self-contained diving suits (allowing Nemo to walk the seafloor) predated the modern **Aqualung** by roughly 70 years.
- **Assassination Attempt:** In 1886, Verne's own nephew shot him twice with a pistol, leaving the author with a permanent limp for the rest of his life.
- **Internet Prediction:** In his 1863 lost novel, *Paris in the Twentieth Century*, Verne predicted a **worldwide network of mechanical calculators** that could communicate with each other.
- **Stockbroker Career:** To support his writing, Verne worked as a highly successful **stockbroker** in Paris, a job he reportedly despised.
- **Experimental Inspiration:** The *Nautilus* was inspired by a real-life French experimental submarine called the **Plongeur**, which Verne saw at the 1867 World's Fair.

- **Simon Lake's Mentor:** Submarine pioneer Simon Lake was so inspired by the book that he credited Verne as the "director-general" of his life.
- **Skywriting:** Decades before it was possible, Verne's stories contained descriptions of **skywriting and video conferencing**.
- **South Pole Error:** In the novel, the *Nautilus* reaches the South Pole by sailing under ice; in reality, the South Pole is located on a **solid continental landmass**.
- **Giant Squid Arms:** Verne incorrectly described his giant squid as having only eight arms, missing the two long feeding tentacles.
- **The Leyden Ball:** Homeland Security later developed a non-lethal stun weapon remarkably similar to the **"Leyden Ball"** electricity bullets Verne imagined.
- **Yankee Stadium Link:** Not a Verne book fact, but his influence was so vast that the first submarine to reach the North Pole in 1958 was named the **USS Nautilus** in his honor.
- **Butchered Translations:** The first 1872 English translation cut nearly **25% of the original text**, removing most of the scientific and political depth.
- **Lentil Fire:** One famous mistranslation rendered Verne's "magnifying lens" (*lentille*) as a **"lentil,"** making it seem like Nemo started a fire with a bean.

- **Ecological Pioneer:** Modern scholars view the character Dr. Aronnax as an early voice for **environmental conservation**, as he frequently criticizes the over-hunting of marine life.
- **Real-Life Mentions:** The book is a blend of fiction and fact, referencing real 19th-century oceanographers like **Matthew Fontaine Maury**.

Thomas Edison's friend Henry Ford allegedly captured his dying breath in a glass test tube. As Edison passed away in 1931, his son Charles was reportedly instructed to seal a tube held near the inventor's mouth at the moment of expiration. While it was likely just one of many open test tubes in the room at the time, Ford—who idolized Edison—kept the tube as a sacred memento of his mentor's "soul," and it remains on display today at the Henry Ford Museum in Michigan.

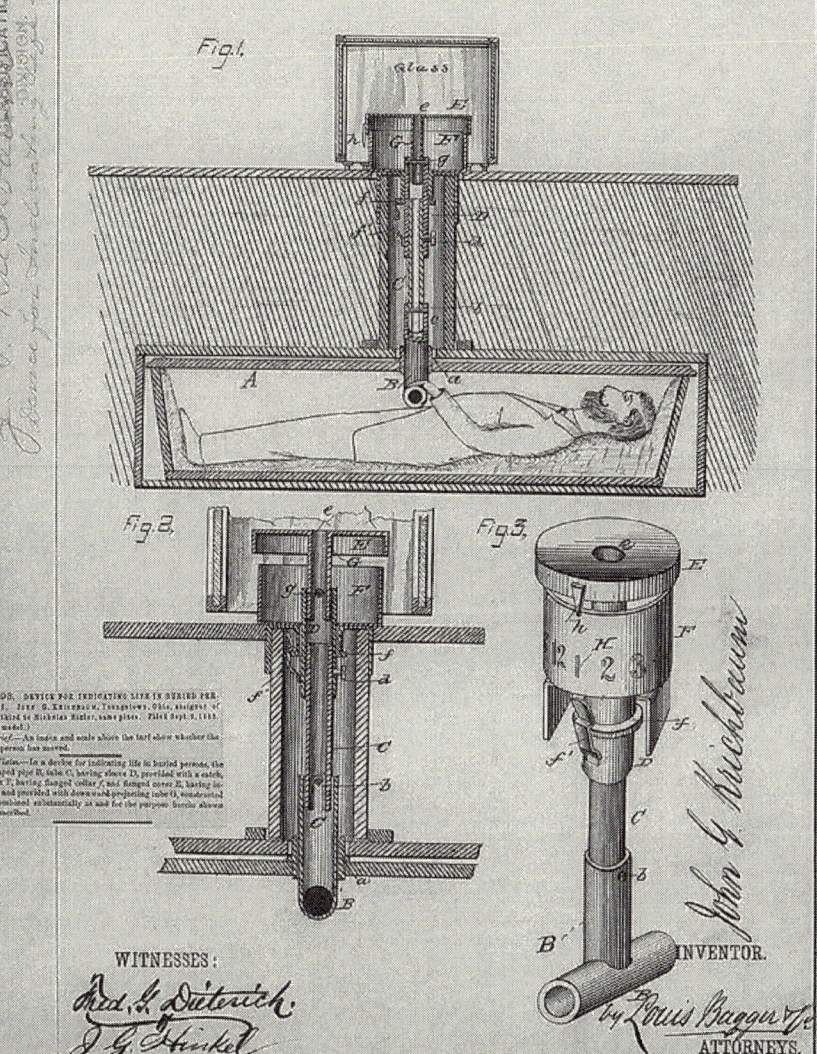

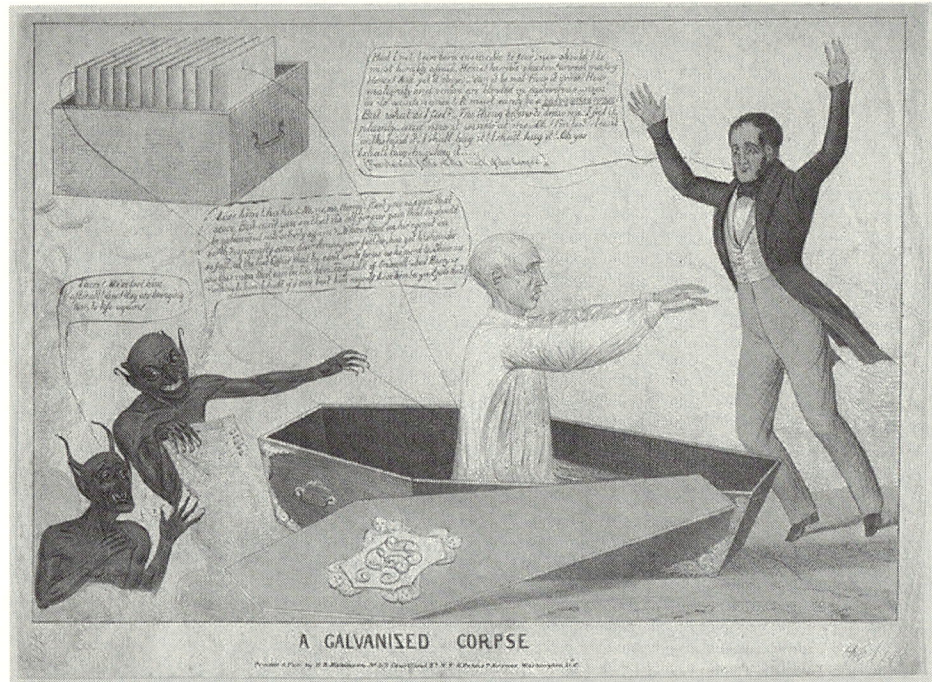

A galvanized corpse refers to a deceased body that has been subjected to galvanism—the 18th- and 19th-century practice of applying electric currents to stimulate muscle contractions. The term originated from the experiments of Luigi Galvani, who discovered in 1780 that electricity could make a dead frog's legs twitch, leading him to believe he had found a vital "animal electricity" that powered life. This concept peaked in 1803 when Galvani's nephew, Giovanni Aldini, performed a famous public demonstration on the corpse of executed murderer George Foster; the electrical stimulation caused the body's jaw to quiver, eyes to open, and limbs to move so violently that witnesses believed it was being resurrected. These "real-life Frankenstein" experiments profoundly influenced Mary Shelley, who cited galvanism as the inspiration for the reanimation of the creature in her 1818 novel Frankenstein. Historically, the term was also used in political satire to describe public figures appearing to "rise from the dead" or being artificially propped up by outside forces.

Orchard Wyndham Stone

The Orchard Wyndham Stone.

The Orchard Wyndham Stone, often referred to as Mother Shipton's Tomb, is a notable landscape feature and pseudo-Roman tombstone located within the grounds of the Orchard Wyndham estate in Somerset, England. Dating to the late 18th or early 19th century, the monument is a physical reconstruction of a genuine Roman funerary altar originally found at Maryport in Cumbria. While the original 1st-century AD Roman marble altar was once part of the private collection at Orchard Wyndham and is now held by the Metropolitan Museum of Art, the outdoor stone remains a celebrated curiosity tied to local folklore. It is traditionally associated with the famous 16th-century English prophetess Mother Shipton, though its actual origins are as a decorative architectural whim of the Wyndham family.

HEDGEHOG VS PORCUIPINE: WHAT ARE THE DIFFERENCES?

While hedgehogs and porcupines both possess protective armor, they are unrelated species whose similarities result from convergent evolution. In 2025, the primary distinction remains their defensive mechanics: porcupines use detachable, barbed quills that lodge into predators, while hedgehogs use non-detachable, barbless spines and a passive "ball-up" defense.

Key Biological Differences

- *Scientific Order:* Porcupines are rodents (Order Rodentia), closely related to beavers and rats. Hedgehogs are insectivores (Order Eulipotyphla), more closely related to shrews and moles.
- *Physical Size:* Porcupines are significantly larger, often reaching 2–3 feet in length and weighing up to 30 pounds or more. Hedgehogs are compact, usually 4–12 inches long and weighing under 3 pounds.
- *Dietary Habits:* Porcupines are strictly herbivores, feeding on bark, fruit, and leaves. Hedgehogs are primarily insectivores or omnivores, eating slugs, worms, insects, and occasionally small amphibians or fruit.

Spine vs. Quill Comparison

Feature	Hedgehog Spines	Porcupine Quills

Attachment	Permanently attached; do not pull out easily	Detach easily upon contact
Structure	Smooth, barbless surface	Barbed tips that hook into flesh
Quantity	Approximately 5,000 to 6,000	Up to 30,000 or more
Length	Usually around 1 inch	Range from 2 to 12+ inches depending on species

Behavioral Differences

- *Defense: When threatened, a hedgehog rolls into a tight, impenetrable ball. A porcupine typically arches its back, rattles its quills, and may swat its tail toward the attacker.*
- *Climbing: Many "New World" porcupines (from the Americas) are excellent climbers with prehensile tails. Hedgehogs are strictly ground-dwelling and do not have tails capable of climbing or balance.*
- *Self-Anointing: Hedgehogs perform a unique "self-anointing" behavior, spreading foamy, often toxic saliva over their spines to deter predators—a behavior not observed in porcupines.*

A mind-blowing and rare fact about the toucan is that its massive beak serves as one of the most efficient thermal radiators in the animal kingdom—functioning much like the ears of an elephant but with even greater precision. Through a process called thermoregulation, a toucan can rapidly expand or contract blood vessels in its uninsulated bill to dump or retain body heat; researchers have observed them changing their beak's temperature by as much as 10°C (18°F) in just a few minutes. This allows them to stay cool in sweltering rainforests without the need to sweat or pant, and it is why they sleep with their beaks tucked under their feathers—to prevent their "radiator" from accidentally draining all their body heat during the cool night

The global "harp sensation" is **Brandee Younger**, a Grammy-nominated musician who has redefined the instrument's role in jazz and hip-hop, recently being named a **Doris Duke Artist** following her acclaimed album *Gadabout Season*. Her work, alongside mainstream performers like **Madison Calley** (who has collaborated with Beyoncé), challenges the 18th-century trope of the harp as a purely "delicate" feminine ornament by showcasing its immense physical and technical demands, such as managing over **2,000 pounds of string tension** and navigating **seven foot-pedals** for chromatic play. Younger's influence extends into the avant-garde, often performing on Alice Coltrane's original restored 1960s harp, while the broader scene includes innovations like "wearable" electronic harps used by artists like **Deborah Henson-Conant** and the continued prominence of international competitions like the **Glowing Harp Festival**, which recently moved its base to Brno.

JIMI

HENDRIX

DIDN'T JUST

PLAY THE GUITAR

—HE WAS THE GUITAR.

— Pete Townshend

In 1969, Jimi Hendrix was actually **kidnapped for a "lost weekend"** after a show in Greenwich Village by thugs demanding his recording contract as ransom, but the guitarist was allegedly so high on drugs during the entire two-day ordeal that he didn't even realize he had been abducted.

Made in the USA
Coppell, TX
20 January 2026

68745834R00016